W9-AAM-852

CARD
TRICKS

Copyright © 2004 Top That! Publishing plc.

an imprint of
SCHOLASTIC
www.scholastic.com

Scholastic and Tangerine Press and associated logos are trademarks of Scholastic Inc.
Published by Tangerine Press, an imprint of Scholastic Inc., 557 Broadway, New York, NY 10012
0-439-68105-7
Printed and bound in China

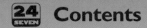

Card tricks may seem easy to perform, but not everyone can do them. To become a magnificent trickster, you need to learn the hints and top card tricks in this book.

Tricks of the Trade

The book is separated into four sections. In the first section, "Tricks of the Trade," you'll learn all the moves you need to know—including how to cut the cards and a sneaky way of shuffling the deck that will fool any audience.

Easy Tricks

Before you try some more complicated tricks, you need to master some easy ones first. Getting the hang of the easy tricks will give you the confidence to confound your audience.

Tricky and Advanced Tricks

When you feel ready, move onto "Tricky Tricks" and "Advanced Tricks." You'll love seeing the confused faces in your audience as people try to discover how you've fooled them. But keep your secrets a secret because you'll enjoy seeing your tricks work over and over again!

Perfect Talk

This is really important! If you wow your audience with words, you will divert their attention from what you are doing with your hands!

Smile!
Smile at them and include lines such as, "Here's a trick that's just a little bit different," or "Now this trick is unbelievable." Humor can be a great distraction because onlookers will find it more difficult to follow what you are doing if they are laughing.

Double Trouble
Never perform the same trick twice in front of the same audience. You don't want them to guess your secrets!

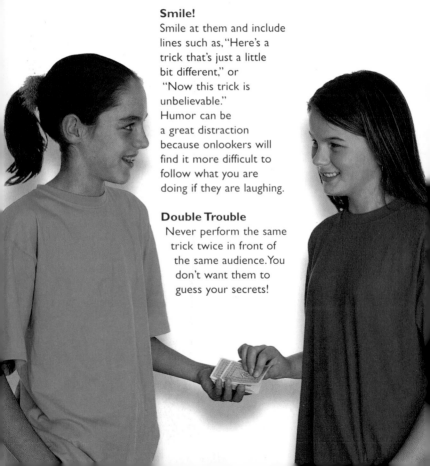

Practice, Practice, Practice

The importance of practice should never be underestimated!

Make It Easy

The more you practice, the more effortless even your most complicated tricks will appear, and it will really boost your confidence when you perform.

As you start to improve, you'll be able to attempt more difficult illusions, and can even start creating your own tricks!

Be Confident

Practice is also important when it comes to shuffling the cards. It may take a little while to feel completely confident holding a deck of cards and shuffling them between your hands. Make sure you can do this with ease before you perform any of the tricks.

Cutting the Cards and Shaping the Fan

Before you can become a real card magician, you need to learn a few basics. Here's a good place to start.

1. Lift off around half the deck and place it to one side.

2. Take what was the bottom half, and put it on top of the other pile. That is cutting the cards.

3. Now it's time to make the deck into a fan shape. Hold the deck in your left hand, making sure your thumb touches the lower end of the deck.

4. Put your right hand on the deck with your fingers at one end and your thumb at the other. Bend the cards over your left forefinger. Move your right hand in a circular motion to the right, letting the cards fan out from your fingers.

5. When all the cards are spread, you have completed the fan shape.

6

Crafty Cut

Make it look as if you have cut the cards when you haven't changed the order at all!

1. Hold the deck in your left hand, and take about half the cards off the bottom with your right hand.

3. Take the top half of the deck in your right hand, moving your right hand slightly upward.

4. Place the cards on top of the ones on the table.

2. Bring the bottom cards toward your body. Now take them over the cards in your left hand, and place them down on the table.

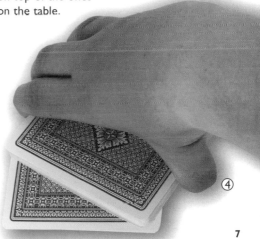

Pick a Card
Force unknowing volunteers to pick the card of your choice!

2. Hold the deck behind your back, and turn around so you are facing away from your audience. Ask a volunteer to take some cards from the top of the deck. When this is done, turn around. As you do this, secretly move the card you remembered from the bottom of the deck to the top.

1. Shuffle the deck, but while you are shuffling, angle the cards so you can sneak a peak at the bottom card. Complete the shuffle, making sure you remember the bottom card.

3. Tell your volunteer that enough cards have been taken. Then say, "Will you take the next card, please?"

4. Then, ask her to hand the card back to you. Taking care not to look at it, hold the card up to your volunteer so that she can see the face.

5. If the card you remembered was, for example, the ace of diamonds, ask your volunteer if that is her card. She will be amazed that you are right!

Overhand Shuffle

All card players use this simple shuffling technique.

1. Hold the cards in your left hand, as in the picture.

3. Put your left thumb on the back of the cards in your right hand, and take some cards off the top of the ones in your right hand.

2. Take most of the bottom half of the cards with your right hand, and lift them over the cards in your left hand.

4. Keep repeating this action until all the cards are in your left hand.

Shuffle Management

Your chosen card will be on top of the deck, even after shuffling!

make sure you don't lose track of the chosen card. Do this by simply making sure it goes from the top of the deck to the bottom.

3. Do another overhand shuffle, but this time keep going until you have only the chosen card in your right hand. Then simply drop it back on top of the deck.

1. Shuffle the cards, and spread them out into a fan. Ask a volunteer to take a card and remember it. Now ask him to put it back, this time on top of the deck.

2. When the chosen card is put back on the deck, give the deck an overhand shuffle (see page 10). When you shuffle,

Feel the Force

This is another way of making someone take the card of your choice.

1. The card that you will force someone to choose is at the bottom of the deck, so before you begin the trick, take a secret look at that card and remember it.

2. Tell a volunteer from your audience that you will force her to choose a card,

and name the card from the bottom of the deck. Hold the cards in your left hand, and place your right hand on top of them, with your right thumb underneath.

3. With the fingers of your right hand, move the cards back a few at a time. Ask your volunteer to say "stop" at any time while you are doing this.

4. Pull back all the cards you have moved with your right hand. At the same time, drag the bottom card with your right thumb so that it is underneath the cards in

your right hand. Hold up these cards to show the bottom one. It is, of course, the card which you told your audience you would find in Step 2.

Spread

You will often need to display all the cards. One way is to spread the cards out evenly on a table.

1. Lay the deck on the table.

2. Lay your right hand flat on top of the deck, making sure your fingers extend beyond the edge of the cards.

3. Push down lightly, and move your hand to the right. The cards will spread out from the bottom, moved by your fingertips.

Pro Tip

This may take some practice, but when you get it right, your routine will be really impressive!

One Good Turn

You'll look very cool with this neat move!

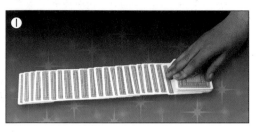

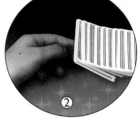

1. Lay the cards face down on a flat surface. Make sure you spread them out evenly. If they are not even, the trick will not work very well.

2. Put your left forefinger under the card farthest to the left.

3. Lift the side of the card up, and then push it over so it is face up. This will make all the other cards turn over as well.

Pro Tip

Practice your tricks on your own first. Then you will really impress your audience when you perform them for real!

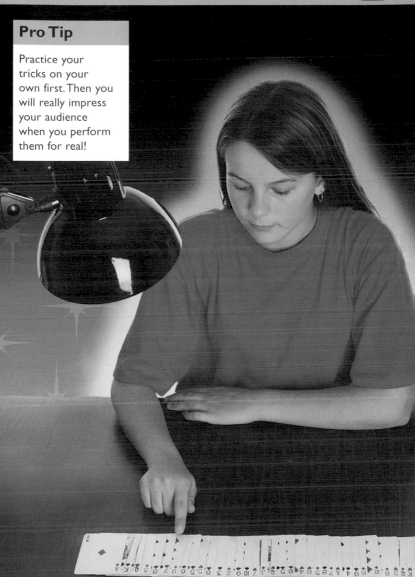

Top Deck

Convince your audience that you have X-ray vision!

(1)

1. Before doing this trick, carefully cut a small window in the card box, so you can see the index corner of the top card.

(3)

2. Shuffle the deck, and return it to its box.

3. Name a card, then remove the deck from the box. The card you named is on the bottom!

4. Amazingly, you are right! Reshuffle the deck, and repeat the trick.

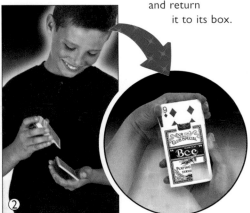

(2)

Vanishing Ace

Make an ace disappear—and then reappear somewhere else, as if by magic!

1. Secretly hide the ace of diamonds somewhere in the room.

3. Turn the cards over, and return them to the deck in different places.

4. Invite a volunteer to take out the ace of diamonds. It's not there!

2. Show the other three aces to your audience, holding them so only the tip of the ace of hearts is showing. Point out to your audience that you are holding the ace of clubs, the ace of diamonds and the ace of spades, and that you are going to make the ace of diamonds disappear.

Shuffle the cards yourself, or pass them to a volunteer to shuffle.

5. Now ask someone else to go to the hiding place. Surprise! There is the missing ace.

King for a Day

You'll need a white candle and some white envelopes for this trick!

Adult Supervision
Always ask an adult for help when using candles.

1. Before you start, ask an adult to light a white candle and drip a little bit of wax on one of the envelopes.

2. Put four jacks, four queens, and a king into nine different envelopes. It doesn't matter which envelopes you put the jacks and queens in, but make sure the king goes in the envelope with the wax on it.

18

3. Ask a volunteer to mix up the envelopes and hand them to you one at a time. By touching the envelopes you will be able to tell when you receive the envelope containing the king.

4. Open the envelope, saying you think it is the one containing the king. Everyone will be amazed by how smooth you are.

Lucky Sixes

Take out all the sixes from the deck—behind your back!

2. Hand out the deck of cards for someone to shuffle for you.

3. Ask for the deck back and hold it behind your back. Announce that you will now remove all four sixes—which you do, with a flourish.

1. Before you start this trick, take out the sixes, and tuck them into your waistband or belt. Later, you will lift them out while you have your hands behind you.

Royal Bag

Find the four kings inside a paper bag!

3. Swiftly put the cards back into the deck, and drop it into the paper bag. Give the bag a good shake.

1. Show the audience an empty paper bag, then remove the four kings from the deck.

2. Fan out the four cards for the audience, secretly clipping them together at the bottom corner with a paper clip. Practice attaching and removing the paper clip smoothly.

4. With a serious "flexing" of magic fingers, declare that you are going to retrieve the four kings.
Put your hand into the bag, feel for the paper clip, and pull out the four cards, ensuring that the paper clip drops back into the bag.

Bottoms Up!

Before you perform this trick, make sure you turn the bottom card of the deck face up.

①

1. Spread the cards face down, and then ask a volunteer to pick a card. When you are doing this, you must conceal the fact that the bottom card is turned up.

2. Ask your volunteer to display the card to the rest of the audience. As you are saying this, transfer the deck from one hand to the other, turning it over at the same time.

③

4. Take the cards behind your back, remove the reversed card, turn it over, and return it to the deck.

5. Put the deck on the table. Turn the cards over one by one, and put them to one side. Say things like, "I'm getting a strong feeling about your card." When you get to the chosen card, it will, of course, already be face up. When you find it, ask, "Is this your card?"

②

3. Ask your volunteer to push their chosen card face down into the deck. Hold the deck firmly so your volunteer doesn't notice that the cards are really face up.

⑤

Surprise Fours

Find a chosen card—and four surprises!

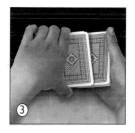

1. Before you start, turn over a five and put it on top of the deck. On top of that, put all the fours, face down.

2. Ask a member of your audience to choose a card. Put it on the bottom of the deck.

3. Cut the deck so the chosen card is now next to the top of the fours.

4. Spread out the cards until you come to the reversed five.

5. Count five cards along, and push out the chosen card. Take away

all the cards to the right of the chosen card and to the left of the five, so you are left with six cards on the table.

6. Reveal the chosen card for the audience to see, and stop as if the trick is finished. Then say, "But here is something more amazing"—and turn up all the fours!

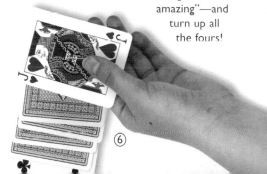

Magic Fingers

Nimble fingers magically sort the cards!

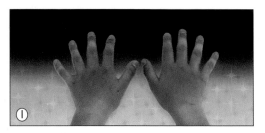

(1)

1. Ask someone to hold out her hands with her fingers touching the table top, just as if she were playing the piano.

2. Take pairs of cards from a deck, and place them between the fingers of each hand, each time saying, "Even."

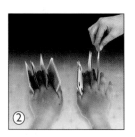

(2)

3. Do this with all the spaces between the fingers, except one. Into this last space, put one card and say, "Odd." The rest of the cards may be put aside.

(4)

4. Take each pair of cards from between the fingers and lay them side by side face down on the table to make two piles, each time again saying, "Even."

5. Now take the single card. Let your volunteer choose which pile to place it on. Tap both piles and say you will now make the "odd" card jump from one pile to the other.

(5)

6. Deal out cards from the chosen pile in pairs, again saying, "Even." Amazingly, it will now be even.

7. Do the same with the other pile, dealing out pairs, and you will be left with one "odd" card, just as you promised!

(7)

Telepathy Test

Demonstrate your baffling powers!

2. Give the rest of the deck to a "volunteer." Explain you will leave the room for a few moments so the audience can choose one of the cards on the table.

3. Return to the room. Pretend to concentrate, then announce the number chosen.

How?

Your volunteer must be your secret assistant. Imagine the deck of cards divided into a grid, matching the one on the table. The assistant holds the deck with her thumb on the spot that corresponds with the position of the card chosen.

1. Shuffle a deck of cards and lay nine cards face up on the table in three rows of three.

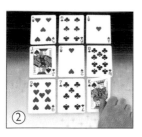

Runaway Couple

Find a pair of cards hidden in the deck!

3. Hold the deck between finger and thumb. Quickly flip the cards so they fly out of your hand, but hold on to the top and bottom cards.

1. Before doing this trick, put the eight of diamonds on the bottom of the deck and the seven of hearts on the top. Return the deck to its box.

2. Hold up the deck, look through it and take out the seven of diamonds and eight of hearts. Hold them up quickly to your audience and say, "I am now going to put these into the center of the deck, and then I will use my amazing powers to find them."

26

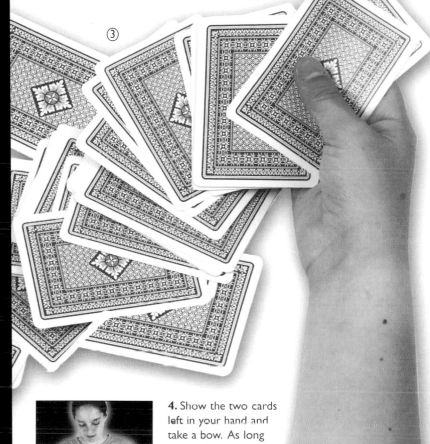

③

4. Show the two cards left in your hand and take a bow. As long as you did not draw attention to the face values, the audience will not notice that the cards have changed.

④

Magic Card Box

All you need is an empty card box and some string for this great trick!

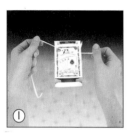
①

1. Loop the string around the outside of the box. Tie a simple overhand knot.

3. As you do this, slide the knot off the box at the same end and push it into the open end. Hold on to the unthreaded string.

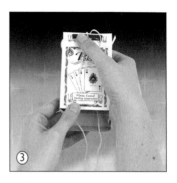
③

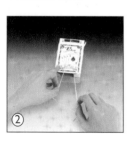
②

2. Push one end of the string into the box and pull it through to the other side.

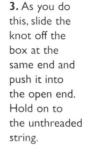

4. As you pull the string through the box, the knot vanishes!

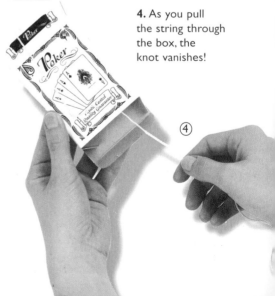
④

Mind Reading

Baffle your audience by reading someone's mind—but the real trick is just a little sleight of hand.

The audience will think that you only have one card left in your pocket, but you know you still have three. Return these two cards to the deck without showing their faces.

1. Before you begin this trick, put any two cards into your pants pocket.

2. Ask a member of your audience to shuffle a deck of cards. Deal the top three cards face up on a table.

3. Memorize the three cards. Then ask your volunteer to think of one of the cards on the table, but not to tell anyone his choice. Pick up the cards, remembering their order, and

carefully put them on top of the other two cards already in your pocket.

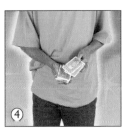

4. Tell your audience that you know which card your volunteer is thinking of. Take out the two cards you hid in your pocket before you began the trick.

5. Ask your volunteer to name his card. Reach into your pocket, and because you memorized the order that you put the cards in, you will be able to easily pull out the chosen card. Your audience will think that you are an amazing mind reader!

Abracadabra!

A magic spell locates a chosen card!

1. Deal three piles of cards, face down, until you have seven in each pile. Set aside the rest of the deck.

2. Ask someone to pick one of the piles.

3. Display the chosen cards in a fan to your volunteer. Ask your volunteer to choose a card but not to tell you what it is.

Pro Tip

This trick only works if you deal three piles at a time, instead of dealing one pile of seven followed by another two piles of seven.

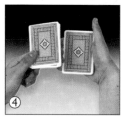

4. Gather up the cards and put the pile containing the chosen card in between the other two piles. Deal the cards in the same way again into three piles of seven.

5. Pick up one pile at a time and display them to the volunteer, asking him to identify the pile which contains his chosen card.

6. Once again, put this pile between the other two, and deal out the cards into three piles.

7. Fan out the cards for a third time. Ask the volunteer to identify the pile containing his card, then put this pile between the other two.

8. Solemnly spell out the word ABRACADABRA, dealing one card for each of the letters spoken out load. Turn over the final card to show it is the chosen one!

Magic Shuffle

Magically deal a line of cards in perfect order!

①

1. You need 10 cards for this trick. Arrange them in advance into this order: eight, three, five, ace, nine, 10, four, six, seven, two.

②

2. Announce you are going to perform a magic shuffle. Hold up the cards and show them to be in a "random" order.

③

3. Put the first card face down on the table. Put the second card at the bottom of the deck in your hand.

4. Put the third card on top of the one on the table, and put the fourth at the bottom of the deck. Continue until all the cards are on the table.

5. Pick up the deck and glance through it with dismay. The trick hasn't worked! You forgot to say the magic words.

6. Perform the same shuffle again, but this time saying some magic words.

⑥

7. Now deal the cards face up in a line on the table. They will be in perfect order.

⑦

The Chosen Card

A card chosen by a member of your audience is lost in the deck, but you can still find it!

I. Ask a member of your audience to shuffle a deck of cards. Now take the deck and ask her to select a card and to show the card she has chosen to the rest of the audience.

2. While she is doing this, quickly and secretly look at the card which is on the bottom of the deck.

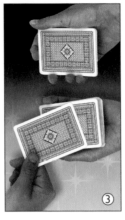

3. Now divide the deck into two. Put the top half of the cards into your left hand. Ask your volunteer to replace her chosen card on top of this half, then put the remaining cards on top of it.

4. The chosen card will now be below the card that you looked at. To make your trick even more convincing, cut the cards again.

5. Spread the deck of cards face up on a magic table. The card chosen by the member of your audience will be on top of the card which was on the bottom of the deck in Step 2.

The Ninth Card

Mystify your audience simply by counting!

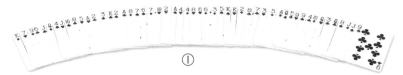

1. Ask a volunteer to shuffle the cards. When they are returned to you, spread the cards face up. Remember the ninth card from the left of the deck. For this example, it is the 10 of spades.

number of cards from the top of the deck one at a time, and place them to one side.

4. Say you will add the two digits of the number. (If the number were 16, the 1 and 6 added together would give you 7.)

5. Now say you think the next card will be the 10 of spades. Ask a volunteer to turn the next card over. Once again, your audience will be stunned!

2. Now put the cards into a pile and pick them up.

3. Ask a volunteer to give you a number between 11 and 18 Then count that

Then remove that number of cards, one by one, from the top of the smaller pile and put them on top of the bigger pile.

Pro Tip

This trick will only work if your volunteer chooses a number between 11 and 18.

Team Game

Before starting this trick, you will need to know the top card of the deck.

1. Shuffle the cards in the way described on page 11.

2. With the cards on your outstretched palm, divide the cards into two piles and balance the top half on your fingers.

them while you look at the top card of the other half.

4. Now place your pile on top of her pile. Pretend to announce the card you looked at, but in fact name the partner of the card you remembered earlier. If the card you memorized was the three of hearts, you say, "Three of diamonds." Everyone will be amazed when the volunteer announces the card she saw. (In this example, it will be the three of hearts.)

3. Ask a volunteer to look at the top card of the pile nearest

Five-Way Split

This trick uses a more complicated method to find a chosen card.

1. Preparation is the key to the success of this trick. Before you start, take all the diamonds from your deck of cards. Count out a pile of 35 cards, and put five diamonds under the pile and another five on top.

2. Give the deck to a member of the audience, and ask him to deal the cards into five piles, face down on the table. Ask him to pick a card from the middle of one of the piles and to remember that card.

3. Tell your volunteer to put the card face down on top of any of the piles. Then ask him to put the piles together to make one deck of cards. Cut the deck several times to make sure his card is well mixed with the others.

4. Spread the deck of cards. To find the right card, slowly scan over the cards. The chosen card will be between two diamonds, so as soon as you see a card splitting two diamonds, you know you have found the right one.

Mind Reading in a Box

Find four chosen cards from the deck without looking!

1. Before you start, put a paper clip in your pocket. Then ask your volunteer to shuffle the deck and then select four cards, which she should memorize.

2. While she is selecting the cards, secretly take the paper clip out of your pocket, and hide it in your left hand.

3. Take the four chosen cards from your volunteer one at a time, and place them in a fan in your left hand. Secretly slide the bottom of each card into the paper clip, which is hidden by your left thumb.

4. Close up the fan of cards. Take the rest of the deck from your volunteer and place the fan on top of the deck. Shuffle the cards to mix them up, treating the four cards in the paper clip as one. Make sure that the paper clip is hidden by keeping it toward your body.

5. Put all of your cards into a box—or even a top hat if you have one!—and shake it. Your audience will think that all of the cards are being mixed together, but you know that the chosen cards are being held together by a paper clip.

6. Say some magical words, then reach into the box and find the four cards. Remove the paper clip, leaving it in the box. Then show that you have found her selected cards!

Pro Tip

When you shuffle the cards, tell a joke or two
divert your audience's attention from what you
are doing.

Back to Back

The key to this trick is to do it quickly. That way, you'll be sure to fool your audience.

1. Hold a card in each hand by its side between your thumb and first finger—the faces should be directly opposite each other. Now position your hands about 12 in. (30 cm) apart.

2. Slowly bring your hands together until each card can be gripped by the thumb and second finger of the opposite hand. There should be a gap of about ½ inch (1.25 cm) between the cards.

3. Raise the cards toward your mouth and tell your audience that you will blow between them, and they will magically change places.

4. As soon as you have blown between the cards, start to move your hands back to their original positions 12 in. (30 cm) apart, the right hand taking the left card, the left hand taking the right card.

Pro Tip

This trick needs a lot of practice before you perform it. Start slowly and gradually build up speed until you can make the change without hesitation. It is the smoothness of your move that will fool your audience.

In the Picture

This trick is so good, have a camera handy to take a picture of your volunteer's face when you've fooled her once again.

1. You'll need two decks of cards for this trick. First, decide which card you are going to force. For this example, let's say it's the seven of spades.

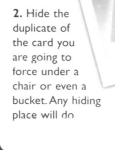

2. Hide the duplicate of the card you are going to force under a chair or even a bucket. Any hiding place will do

3. Take the deck of cards and "force" (see page 8) your volunteer to choose the card that is hidden.

4. When the card has been chosen, ask your volunteer to look under the bucket. She will be bewildered when she sees that the card is the same as the one she chose!

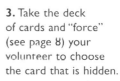

④

Mega Mind Reading

What's better than reading one person's mind? Reading two, of course!

1. Prepare your trick. Take any card, and on its back put one pencil dot in the top left-hand and bottom right-hand corners. Put this card in your pocket until you are ready to use it.

2. Shuffle the deck of cards, then ask two volunteers to select a card each, which they need to remember without telling anyone.

3. While they are remembering their cards, secretly retrieve the marked card from your pocket and put it on the bottom of the deck.

4. Ask one of your volunteers to replace her card on top of the deck. Cut the deck. Place the top half of the cards in your left hand, then put the other half on top. The marked card is now on top of the first chosen card.

5. Spread the deck face down to find your marked card. Cut the deck in half one card below the marked card, then put the top half of cards underneath the other half. This takes the first chosen card to the bottom of the deck, with the marked card above it. Quickly look at the bottom card and remember it.

6. Ask your second volunteer to replace his card on the top of the deck. Cut the deck as you did in Step 4 to bring the first and second chosen cards and the marked card together.

7. Announce to your audience that you will now read your first volunteer's mind! Make a big show of

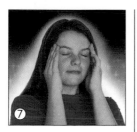

concentrating hard, closing your eyes and breathing deeply. Then reveal the name of the chosen card (which you found in Step 5), ask your volunteer to confirm that this is the right one, and your audience will gasp.

8. They will be even more amazed when you complete the trick and read a second person's mind. To do this, spread the deck of cards in front of you. The second chosen card will be on top of the first chosen card. Of course, now that you know the secret of how to read two minds at once, there's no reason why you can't read three, four, or even five!

Flipper

A chosen card finds itself by turning in midair!

1. Find a chosen card (see page 32). Tell your audience that you are going to make the chosen card flip itself over. While you are doing this, secretly cut the card to the top of the deck.

3. With your right hand, lift the deck up, then throw it straight down into your left hand.

2. Holding the deck in your left hand, bring your right hand over the cards. While you are doing this, push the top card slightly to the right with your left thumb.

4. Your audience will be amazed as the chosen card flips over in midair, and then lands on top of the deck!

52-Card Scatter

This is a spectacular way to find a chosen card—but it takes nerve!

1. Start by losing and then finding a chosen card (see page 32). Secretly cut the card to the top of the deck.

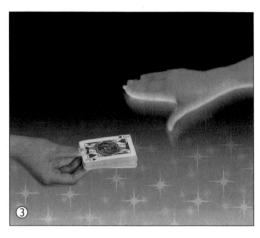

2. Now ask a member of your audience to hold her hand out, palm upward. Then position the deck face up in her hand so that her fingers stretch underneath the cards for at least 1 inch (2.5 cm) and about ½ inch of her thumb is on the top of the deck. Ask her to hold the deck firmly.

3. This step requires nerves of steel! Strike down with your hand on the end of the deck that is not being held.

4. All the cards will scatter to the floor, except the chosen card, which is being held firmly between the fingers and thumb of your volunteer.

④

Magic Spell

The secret to this trick is to spell it out!

1. Before you start the trick, remove and arrange thirteen cards as follows: three, eight, seven, ace, queen, six, four, two, jack, king, ten, nine, and five. Put these on top of the deck.

3. Take the thirteen cards from the top, and spread them in a fan face down.

4. Now, here comes the tricky part. Spell out the word "ace"

and, as you do this, remove one card from the top of the deck for each letter and place it on the bottom. Then turn over the fourth card. It will be the ace!

5. Do the same for each card. You must do it in this order— ace, two, three, four, five, six, seven, eight, nine, ten, jack, queen, king—for the trick to work.

2. Shuffle the cards, but make sure the thirteen cards from Step1 remain at the top of the deck.

Aces High

Play a trick without even touching the cards.

1. Before performing the trick, place the four aces on top of the deck.

2. Ask a volunteer to cut the deck into two piles. Keep track of which pile the aces are in.

3. Now ask the volunteer to cut the two piles into two more piles so you now have four piles. The aces should be on one of the end piles.

4. Ask your volunteer to take three cards from the pile farthest away from the pile containing the aces. The volunteer should then put these cards at the bottom of the pile. Then ask him to deal the top three cards, one at a time, onto each of the other three piles.

5. The volunteer should then do the same with the other three piles in sequence. But make sure that the last pile to be dealt is the one containing the aces.

6. Now when you turn over the top card of each pile, the four aces will be revealed.

Pointing Exercise

You'll need to use your thumb for this sleight of hand!

1. Ask a volunteer to shuffle a deck of cards and then remove a few.

②

③

2. Take the chosen cards and fan them out so that they are facing toward another volunteer. Ask the second volunteer to point at a card.

3. Although you can't see the faces of the cards, you will know the identity of the card chosen. This is because you use your left thumb to push up the bottom corner of the card so you can see the index.

4. Announce the card your volunteer has chosen. He will be astounded by your mind-reading power.

④

Back to Front

Before performing this trick, place the six of any suit face up in the sixth position from the bottom of the deck.

1. Ask a volunteer to pick a card from your fan and remember it. When you are doing this, make sure you don't expose the reversed card.

2. Your volunteer should now place the chosen card on the bottom of the deck.

3. Cut the deck a few times until the card is somewhere in the middle of the deck.

4. Announce that this trick is too easy and that you have decided to turn one of the cards in the deck over as well as finding your

volunteer's card. Spread the cards face down across the table until the reversed card becomes visible. Then turn over the sixth card to the left of the six. This will be your volunteer's card.

Here you will find explanations for terms in the book that you may not be familiar with, and also some other terms that you may come across while using playing cards.

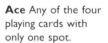

Ace Any of the four playing cards with only one spot.

Cut Dividing the deck into two random parts after shuffling.

Fan The shape in which dealt cards are usually held in the hand, or the shape in which they are usually placed on the table.

Index the symbol in the corner that shows which card it is.

Force Tricking someone into picking the card you want him to without his knowledge.

Joker A card that does not belong to any suit, nor does it have a number. It can be used in some games and tricks, but it is not always required.

Overhand shuffle A basic shuffle.

Royal Any of the jacks, queens, or kings.

Shuffle Mixing up the deck to change the order of the cards.

Suit Any of the four sets of 13 cards: clubs, diamonds, hearts, or spades.